Cass R. Sandak

BENJAMIN FRANKLIN

Richard B. Morris, Consulting Editor

Franklin Watts   1986   A First Book
New York   London   Toronto   Sydney

To Franklin

Photographs courtesy of: The Bettmann Archive:
opposite p. 1, pp. 10, 15, 19, 22, 26, 32, 38, 56;
The New York Public Library Picture Collection:
p. 45; Culver Pictures, Inc.: p. 51

Library of Congress Cataloging in Publication Data
Sandak, Cass R.
Benjamin Franklin
(A First book)
Bibliography: p.
Includes index.
Summary: A biography of the eighteenth-century printer,
inventor, and statesman who played an influential
role in the early history of the United States.
1. Franklin, Benjamin, 1706–1790—Juvenile
literature.   2. Statesmen—United States—Biography—
Juvenile literature.   3. United States. Constitution—
Juvenile literature. [1. Franklin, Benjamin, 1706–1790.
2. Statesmen] I. Title.
E302.6.F8S28   1986   973.3'092'4   [B]   [92]   86-1641
ISBN 0-531-10107-X

Contents

Benjamin Franklin

A 1777 engraving of Benjamin Franklin,
with coonskin cap and bifocals

Introduction

A Many-Sided Man

Everyone knows of something that Benjamin Franklin has left behind: a famous saying from *Poor Richard's Almanack*, information about how he "discovered" electricity with the kite and key, how he made printing an exciting art, how he invented bifocals—the famous "half" reading glasses—or even the fur hat that he wears in so many portraits. He was that kind of person. His influence was great, and he made a lasting impression upon America and the world.

It is harder to understand the man himself, a man who played so many different roles amid the turmoil of the emerging American nation. Franklin was a man whose lifespan (1706–1790) covered all but a few years of the whole eighteenth century. It was against the backdrop of early America that Benjamin Franklin played out the richest of lives.

Benjamin Franklin was unique not only in the exceptional breadth of his interests, but also in the depth in which he pursued them. He made significant contributions to civilization in an amazing number of fields. His achievements are particularly noteworthy since Franklin had not enjoyed the benefits of a formal education. Except for two years in grammar school, he was completely self-educated. Through reading, through discussions with skilled and learned people, and by keen observation of and reflection on everything in the world around him, Franklin was able to become one of the most cultivated people of his—or any other—time.

Fifty-four of Franklin's eighty-four years were spent in public life, serving in a number of different capacities, many of them simultaneously. While continuing to maintain an interest in his many business ventures, he managed to become involved in a significant way in almost all the important events of his time.

The fame that surrounds a great man can make him seem unreal and unapproachable. All too often we see only the public side of the man. But Franklin left writings that reveal a lot about himself, and in them we see the most human of men. In his writings and in his conversation, Franklin constantly gave advice on living wisely and virtuously. But he also recognized his own faults and weaknesses and was always trying to correct them.

Franklin had a good sense of humor and was frequently able to laugh at himself. In one of the most endearing passages from his autobiography, he tells how ridiculous he looked when as a boy of seventeen he first arrived in Philadelphia. He was hungrily stuffing bread into his mouth and carrying two more loaves under his arm when he first caught sight of Deborah Read, the woman who would later become his wife.

Franklin was a very warm and real person. His good spirits were even able to carry him through difficult and tragic times, as when his son, Francis, died of smallpox at the age of four. On one of his extended stays in England, Franklin befriended some neighborhood children. As a present for them, he had a squirrel imported from Pennsylvania as a pet. When the squirrel, named Skugg, died, Franklin penned a bittersweet epitaph: "Here lies Skugg, as snug as a bug in a rug."

Franklin loved all children, but especially his grandchildren. During his final illness, he kept a jar of jam by his bedside and rewarded his granddaughter with a spoonful of it after she had recited her school lessons.

Franklin was able to be at home in many different circumstances and in many different places. He had the ability to be comfortable with all levels of people—rich and powerful or poor and humble. He was born to modest beginnings but achieved greatness through sheer force of character. In any time period it is likely he would have succeeded in making his mark upon the age.

Franklin's life was full of high points. He was acclaimed for achievements in science and invention, in education, in printing and literature, in politics, and in the struggle of international diplomacy. In his twilight years he came to the Constitutional Convention an honored elder statesman whose knowledge and years of experience were greatly admired.

During his lifetime, Benjamin Franklin was active in many fields and involved in many events that were to become part of the history of the budding nation. And he made many lasting contributions to philosophy, literature, and science, as well as to the American way of life.

1

A Boy in Boston

Benjamin Franklin was born on January 17, 1706. He was the fifteenth of his father's seventeen children and his father's tenth son. One of the very first events in the newborn child's life was being carried in his father's arms from the house in Milk Street to Boston's Old South Meeting House to be christened.

Benjamin was named for one of his uncles, his father's brother in England. In the eighteenth century, babies were baptized as soon as possible. In those days many infants died shortly after birth and it was important to ensure the divine blessing on the immortal soul of a baby, whose body might all too soon be called back to his Creator. Josiah Franklin also had something else in mind, since he had decided to offer this child to the service of the Almighty by preparing him for a career as a Congregational minister.

Franklin's mother was Abiah Folger, who came from Nantucket Island, off the coast of Massachusetts. His father, Josiah, had come to America from England in 1682 or 1683, leaving behind brothers and other family members.

In later years, when Franklin was living in England and acting as colonial agent for Pennsylvania, he searched out his father's English relatives. He traced the Franklin family's origins to Ecton (in Nottinghamshire) and researched the family tree back to 1555. He had to stop there; records of births, deaths, marriages, and baptisms in the parish church only extended back that far.

Growing Up in Puritan Boston

The Franklins were Congregationalists, a Protestant sect that favored simplicity and fostered godliness, good works, and self-reliance. Josiah was an elder, or an elected officer, of the nearby Congregational church, and singing hymns was one of his favorite pastimes. The city of Boston was a part of the Massachusetts Bay Colony, which had been founded and settled by strict Protestant sects.

No doubt the Franklins kept many of the customs of their Puritan neighbors. Cooking on Sunday was frowned upon, so the family usually followed the New England tradition of warming up a big pot of baked beans and brown bread that had been baked the day before. Games and boisterous entertainments were frowned upon, too, on the Sabbath, and young Ben Franklin very early developed the habit of devoting Sundays to study and reading books of an improving nature. To him this way of spending the day was infinitely preferable to wearying the mind and body sitting in church for services that in those days could last three or four hours.

Among His Father's Books

The Franklin household, however modest, was a literate one where books were prized. Reading was done both for instruction and amusement. Franklin learned to read at such an early age that later in life he said he could not remember a time when he could not read. Among the books that Franklin read as a boy were Daniel Defoe's works—*Robinson Crusoe* and *A Journal of the Plague Years*—and John Bunyan's *The Pilgrim's Progress*, a story of Christian life. In his autobiography Franklin tells us he first encountered these books in his father's small but select personal library.

Franklin taught himself to write well by studying the works of writers that he admired. He took notes on an essay, for example, put them aside, and then later tried to re-create the piece from memory.

In addition to his efforts at reading and self-improvement, Franklin did have some formal schooling. For two years he attended a Boston grammar school. At the age of ten, when his schooling ended, Franklin went to work in his father's shop. He continued his efforts at self-education, as he was to do throughout his life.

Childhood Games

Even in the eighteenth century children liked to play, and Benjamin Franklin was no exception. Franklin was an active child who enjoyed playing games and climbing trees. He liked to fish and canoe, and he early learned to swim in Boston harbor. Franklin used his inventive spirit even when he was a child. Before swimming, he tied paddles to his hands and feet to make his progress in the water faster and easier. He also liked to float on his back while a high-flying kite pulled him along.

But playtime also provided learning experiences. Franklin early learned the lesson that crime does not pay. He and his friends were scolded when they took some building stones to make a small fishing pier for themselves.

Boston's waterfront was a favorite spot because ships arriving from England always created a lot of excitement. It is not surprising that for many years Franklin dreamed of becoming a sailor.

The Franklin Household

In earlier times children were expected to help their parents in any way possible. There was always a lot of work to do in an age when so many aspects of life were harder. Electricity and other modern conveniences did not exist. Wood for cooking and for fuel had to be ready for use in the house every day. Without indoor plumbing, water for drinking and washing had to be carried in from a well. In a large family everyone had to pitch in and help with the countless chores.

Franklin's father was a candle- and soapmaker. From an early age Benjamin was expected to assist his father in the shop making and selling the candles and soap that were the family's livelihood. Josiah Franklin was able to provide well for his family although they could by no means be considered well-to-do. Their way of life was modest, but it was firmly middle class in its values and outlook.

The elder Franklin hoped to send Benjamin to Harvard College, across the Charles River in Cambridge, to be educated for the ministry. After turning this plan over in his mind, however, he decided to abandon it. A college education was expensive and a minister's salary was often inadequate. Mr. Franklin therefore decided that it would be best if he prepared his son to be a tradesman like himself. But young Benjamin disliked his father's trade intensely Both father and son looked for other ways for the boy to make a living.

Franklin the Apprentice

In 1718, at the age of twelve, young Benjamin Franklin was apprenticed to his older half-brother, James (1697–1735), a printer who had learned his trade in England. The system of apprenticeship had been developed during the Middle Ages as the accepted method of training craftsmen.

As an apprentice Franklin learned all about the printing trade—and there was much to learn. Today, printing is done on automatic presses from printing plates that are produced by a photographic process. Type is set automatically, usually by computer. In Franklin's time, printing was an art that required many different skills that could be mastered only by experience. Each metal letter was selected from a tray and was stacked, letter by letter, one line at a time, onto a composing stick. Once the type was placed on the bed of the printing press, sticky black ink was spread over the type with leather balls or rollers. Handmade sheets of paper were put on a frame and then placed in the printing press, which was operated by a giant screw turned by a lever.

The printed sheets then had to be proofread. Proofreading is the careful reading of a trial sheet, or "proof," which is the first page printed from the newly set type. Smudges and errors may be corrected by adjusting the type on the press before the final printing is done. Franklin spent long days working in the shop or selling the newspapers that were printed there.

Young Benjamin Franklin mastered all of the necessary skills, and within two years he was largely responsible for his brother's newspaper, the *New-England Courant*. While working on the paper, Franklin engaged in some of his earliest literary ventures. These included a series of letters supposedly written by a widowed lady, Mrs. Silence Dogood. The Dogood letters were essays that com-

Franklin began his publishing career in Boston at his brother's newspaper, the New-England Courant.

bined humorous and serious commentary on life in New England. Franklin wrote the letters in secret and then slid them under the shop door at night to avoid detection. His brother published the letters, and they helped to make the newspaper popular.

But it appears that James Franklin was not cautious enough in exercising editorial control over the paper he published. In 1722 James was jailed for a month for printing stories that were thought libelous of the British authorities (libel is the written form of slander). While James was in prison, Benjamin ran the paper.

When James was released from jail, the colonial authorities forbade him to continue publishing his paper. Benjamin was named as the paper's publisher, although his brother remained in control. He and Benjamin frequently quarreled over the content of the paper.

Franklin was tired of living in his brother's shadow and he saw the chance to assert his independence. Soon Benjamin decided to leave his brother's employ to seek work elsewhere. Franklin had not fulfilled all of the terms of his apprenticeship agreement, having served only five years of a period that normally lasted nine years. But he had learned enough of the printer's trade to be confident of finding work in another printshop. And eventually he hoped to set up a business of his own.

With money he had obtained by selling some of his books, young Franklin sailed from Boston to New York City, where he hoped to find work. But he discovered that a recent opening for a printer had just been filled. New York in those days was smaller than Boston, and there was no need for another printer. He heard that there might be an opening in Philadelphia, so he set off for that city.

2

A Philadelphia Printer and Writer

In 1723 Philadelphia was the second largest city in the American colonies (after Boston). It was separated from New York by about 100 miles (160 km) of New Jersey forest and farmland. After taking a boat part of the way, Franklin walked most of the last 50 miles (80 km). He arrived in Philadelphia on a Sunday morning in October, tired, hungry, and nearly penniless. His best clothes— and virtually the only clothes he owned—were stained with mud and perspiration. He made himself as presentable as he could and set out to apply for the opening he had heard about.

For a period of time Franklin worked for a kindly but eccentric Philadelphia printer named Samuel Keimer. Soon after Franklin arrived in Pennsylvania, the royal governor of the colony, Sir William Keith, met the young printer and was so impressed with his intelligence and ambition that he offered to set him up in a business of his own. He also offered to pay Franklin's expenses to travel to London to buy the printing press, type, and other equipment necessary for opening a printing shop.

Before going abroad, Franklin returned to Boston to visit his family. His parents readily forgave him for leaving his apprenticeship, but his brother James was still bitter. The main purpose of the visit was to ask his father for funds for opening his own shop. But Josiah Franklin thought that his eighteen-year-old son was still too young and refused to advance the money.

Just before Benjamin left Boston, the Franklins' old minister, the famous writer and preacher Cotton Mather, gave him a special blessing, but cautioned the headstrong young man always to be humble, especially when he was tempted to be proud. Mather's words stayed with Franklin throughout his life.

Young Franklin set off eagerly for London at his own expense, only to have the governor change his mind and refuse to pay. Franklin found himself in London with little money and no friends. He soon remedied both situations, however, by going to work for another printer and quickly making a number of acquaintances. He stayed in London about a year and half, from late in 1724 until 1726, and then returned to Philadelphia, a well-trained and highly skilled printer.

His First Printshop

Franklin worked briefly for other printers before acquiring his own shop, the New Printing Office, in partnership with Hugh Meredith. In 1729 he bought out Meredith's interest and became the sole proprietor. That same year he purchased the *Pennsylvania Gazette* and turned it into the most popular newspaper in the colonies. The newspaper had been founded in 1728 by Franklin's former employer, Samuel Keimer.

As a master printer, Franklin prospered. He had the first copperplate press in the United States, which he used for printing bank notes. He was also the first printer to mold type from lead forms.

Franklin tried to arouse interest in a German-language newspaper to serve Philadelphia's large immigrant population, but the attempt failed. Throughout his career, Franklin was a champion of free speech and freedom of the press. He stated, "If all printers were determined not to print anything until they were sure it would offend nobody, there would be very little printed."

Franklin's first print jobs were mostly commercial handbill advertisements and business forms for other merchants. But he soon began to do much of the official printing for the government of Pennsylvania and to publish his own writings. As his business expanded, Franklin established printing offices and other business connections throughout the colonies.

Franklin continued as a printer for more than thirty years before selling his business. Over the years his printing shop in Philadelphia had expanded into a combination bookstore, general store, post office, and grocery. Patrons could buy soap, wax candles, nails, paper, cheeses, and hundreds of other assorted goods as well as a selection of books and pamphlets, many of them imported from England.

Marriage and Family Life

After Franklin had established himself as a successful printer with his own business, he felt he was ready to take on the responsibilities of maintaining a wife and family.

In 1730, when he was twenty-six, Benjamin Franklin asked his old friend Deborah Read to be his wife. He had known her for

*Five years after Franklin arrived in Philadelphia, he had
his own newspaper, the Pennsylvania Gazette. He was 23.*

about seven years, ever since he first came to Philadelphia. Deborah Read was a simple woman with no education. She could barely read or write, but she was a good and devoted wife. They were a happy couple. Together Benjamin and Deborah Franklin raised three children, one of whom, Francis, died at age four. William and Sarah lived to become adults and establish families of their own.

Deborah was a thrifty housewife, a good mother, and a hard worker in the shop that provided the family's livelihood. Although pressing business often kept Benjamin and Deborah apart for long periods—sometimes years at a time—the two were very devoted to each other. They kept track of each other's lives in a lively correspondence that is very touching to read. When Benjamin was in England for years at a time, Deborah sent him foods from back home, things like home-cured bacon, venison, cranberries, and yellow cornmeal. Franklin sent back yards of silk and other materials for dresses, porcelain dishes from the famous English pottery makers, and even a useful kitchen device that he found in a London shop—an apple corer.

Deborah died in 1774 during one of Franklin's long trips abroad. After her death, Franklin wrote of Deborah that she had been "a good and faithful helpmate. . . . We throve together and mutually endeavored to make each other happy."

Franklin the Practical Man

As a young man, and indeed throughout his life, Franklin was interested in saving money. At first he wanted to build a nest egg and to set himself up in business. To these ends he was very careful with the money he spent. And he cautioned others to avoid debt. He believed that any man could achieve a measure of economic success by hard work and thrift.

For a period of time he practiced vegetarianism long before it became fashionable. Both for health reasons and for economy he practiced moderation in food and drink and made a habit of drinking water with his meals. He believed a light diet promoted clearheadedness and helped prevent disease. Eventually he gave up vegetarianism, but he always tried to limit the amount of meat he ate.

Franklin attributed his habits of thrift to his New England upbringing. In a large family with a small income, care had to be taken to make every penny go as far as possible. In his autobiography Franklin recalled a childhood incident that taught him the value of money. After being given a few pennies, he went out and bought a whistle that had caught his eye. However, he ended up paying four times what the toy was worth. His family laughed at him when they discovered how much he had paid. The embarrassment he felt far exceeded the joy he received from the whistle. The lesson was one that he never forgot.

Franklin was careful to accumulate wealth not for its own sake, nor even for the things it could buy. But he prized money both because it was useful for helping others and because it gave him the freedom to pursue his other interests, mainly science, politics, and civic improvement. He was very generous and gave or lent money to friends, relatives, acquaintances, and organizations that needed it.

Franklin the Writer

As a printer and the publisher of the *Pennsylvania Gazette*, Franklin had ample opportunity to see much of his own writing in print. His publishing ventures earned him acclaim, popularity, and wealth. In addition to regular contributions to his own newspaper, he was also the author of occasional articles and pamphlets independently circulated. Franklin taught himself a lively and straightforward style in imitation of the great British essayists, particularly Joseph Addison and Richard Steele.

Franklin was easily the greatest American writer of the eighteenth century. His writing generally addressed some particular issue, and the clear purpose behind his work is one of the strong points of his writings as well as one of the reasons he wrote so well.

Franklin valued hard work and common sense, and these ideas shine through his writing. He also attempted with his political essays and pamphlets to influence public opinion on topics of current interest. For example, he was keenly interested in Indian affairs and in seeing that Native Americans were treated fairly and not cheated out of their ancestral lands.

Franklin set great store by his ability as a writer. When he set out to plan his autobiography, "my writing" was the first entry on his outline of topics to include. He credited much of his success in public life to his ability to think and write clearly, especially as he recognized that he was not an effective public speaker. He preferred to write out prepared statements of his thoughts and then read them when the time came to present his arguments.

Poor Richard's Almanack

From 1732 to 1757 Franklin wrote and published *Poor Richard's Almanack,* a collection of weather and calendar forecasts, jokes, stories, and proverbs. It was called Poor Richard's after the name of the imaginary author Richard Saunders, a henpecked husband and armchair philosopher. Almanacs were soft-cover books that were immensely popular in early America. They were instructive, they were helpful, and they were cheap. Nearly every household purchased a copy, and in many homes it was the only other book besides the Bible.

Poor Richard, 1733.

AN

Almanack

For the Year of Chrift

1 7 3 3,

Being the Firft after LEAP YEAR.

And makes fince the Creation	**Years**
By the Account of the Eaftern *Greeks*	7241
By the Latin Church, when ☉ ent. ♈	6932
By the Computation of *W.W.*	5742
By the *Roman* Chronology	5682
By the *Jewifh* Rabbies.	5494

Wherein is contained

The Lunations, Eclipfes, Judgment of the Weather, Spring Tides, Planets Motions & mutual Afpects, Sun and Moon's Rifing and Setting, Length of Days, Time of High Water, Fairs, Courts, and obfervable Days.

Fitted to the Latitude of Forty Degrees, and a Meridian of Five Hours Weft from *London*, but may without fenfible Error, ferve all the adjacent Places, even from *Newfoundland* to *South Carolina*

By *RICHARD SAUNDERS*, Philom.

PHILADELPHIA:
Printed and fold by *B. FRANKLIN*, at the New Printing-Office near the Market

Franklin did not originate all of the wise and pithy sayings that appear on the pages of *Poor Richard*. He took many of them from the literature and folklore of the world. In other instances, Franklin expressed his own philosophy and summed up the wisdom of generations. Many times the phrases were reworked and reworded for inclusion in later issues of *Poor Richard*. The decision to publish *Poor Richard's Almanack* helped insure Franklin's financial success. At its peak, more than 10,000 copies were sold throughout the colonies each year.

The Autobiography

Franklin began to write the story of his life when he was sixty-five and living in England. Even though many of the events he wrote about had taken place more than a half century before, he could recall them vividly and still write about them entertainingly. Franklin wrote down a detailed and continuous story of his entire life and of the things that influenced the development of his mind and thought. No one had really tried this before in such a comprehensive and unified way. Franklin may almost be said to have invented and popularized a new literary form: the autobiography.

The autobiography was the one lengthy work that Franklin wrote. He was not able to tell as much of the story of his life as he had wanted to, but the large portion of it that was completed is a gem of entertaining and honest self-portrayal.

It is interesting to note that the autobiography was published first in French in Paris in 1791, the year following Franklin's death. The earliest English edition came out in 1793 in London. It was an English translation of the French edition! It was not until 1868 that a version of the book taken from the original manuscript, written in English and in Franklin's own hand, was printed.

3

The Scientist and Inventor

By 1748 Franklin had prospered to the extent that he was content to turn the management of his printing and book-selling business over to others. This maneuver gave him more time to devote to other interests, such as politics and philanthropy. It also left him free to indulge his passion for science.

Natural philosophy was the name often applied to the study of science in the eighteenth century. Natural philosophers tried to uncover the secrets of the natural world by careful observation, by experiment, and by the use of logic—in short, by the scientific method.

Investigating Electricity

In one of the most famous experiments of all time, Franklin proved that lightning and static electricity represented the same force. Franklin was the first among several scientists of the mid-eighteenth

As a scientist, Franklin is best known for
his experiments in electricity.

century who tried to understand the nature of the force we call electricity. He devised experiments to test his hypotheses. Franklin had set out to prove what he called his "one-fluid" theory of electricity when he designed his famous kite and key experiment. The experiment was successful in demonstrating the way an electric current "flowed" in a continuous path from a storm cloud into a waiting Leyden jar, a primitive type of battery first devised at Leyden, in the Netherlands.

During a thunderstorm in 1752 Franklin flew a silk kite fitted with a pointed metal rod. A bluish current of electricity traveled down the wet kite string to an iron key that conducted the electricity into the Leyden jar. Later Franklin attached a wire to the jar and used the stored electricity to ring a bell.

Because electricity was such an unknown force, Franklin had no idea of its great power and how dangerous his experiment actually was. He took some precautions. He had the foresight to hold the key by a silk ribbon. This insulated him from the electricity and thus probably saved his life. Also, Franklin's kite string probably did not conduct an actual lightning bolt but merely a much less powerful electrical discharge. A lightning bolt probably would have killed him instantly. Others who have tried to reproduce his experiment have been killed or injured in the process.

In this famous experiment, Franklin proved that lightning and electricity are the same thing. Based on his discovery, Franklin invented the lightning rod to protect buildings against the dangers of fire caused by lightning striking them. The lightning rod is a metal rod mounted on top of a house, a barn, a church steeple, or other high building and attached by a wire to the ground. Lightning striking the building is conducted through the metal rod and cable to the ground where it becomes harmless.

In 1752 Franklin sent his first scientific paper on electricity to the Royal Society of London for the Improvement of Natural Knowledge. The Society had been founded in 1662 and promoted scientific inquiry by encouraging scientists to share their discoveries through meetings and publications. Prominent naturalists in England, America, and Europe belonged to the Society. Franklin became a member and received recognition from leading scientists throughout the world.

Other Investigations

Franklin was interested in all kinds of natural phenomena. On one of his Atlantic crossings, he plotted the course of the Gulf Stream, the current of warm water that runs across the Atlantic Ocean. The stream influences the climate of the British Isles and the rest of northwestern Europe by carrying warm waters from the Gulf of Mexico eastward across the Atlantic Ocean to Europe. At intervals Franklin suspended a thermometer over the side of the ship and took temperature readings. The ship roughly followed the course of the stream and Franklin was fascinated by the way the water remained warm even as it passed through ocean waters that were many degrees cooler.

Franklin made other systematic studies of heat absorption and weather predictions. He improved the design and construction of chimneys, and pioneered the use of mineral fertilizers to increase crop yields.

Franklin the Inventor

Franklin was adept at problem solving. When he saw a need for something, he speedily found a way to meet that need. This adaptability carried over into the field of invention. What Franklin found a need for he invented.

Franklin invented bifocal spectacles when he found that he needed two separate pairs of glasses—one for seeing nearby objects and one for seeing distant things. Even at the dinner table he noted that if he could see the food on his plate clearly he could not see the face of the person sitting across from him. He therefore had a glass cutter slice the lenses of each pair of glasses in half. The halves of different lenses were clamped together, with the lower halves for close work and the upper halves for distance vision. Franklin thereby could use one pair of glasses for two purposes.

In 1743 Franklin invented the heating device known as the Franklin stove. At first it was a boxlike iron fireplace that could be inserted inside an existing fireplace. The stove made more efficient use of fuel than an ordinary fireplace, where much of the heat went up the chimney and was wasted. The iron sides of the stove heated up and radiated heat, which warmed roughly twice as much space in the room as an open fire. Grates, sliding doors, and heating panels improved the stove's efficiency. Over the years various improvements were made to what came to be known as the Pennsylvania fireplace. For more than a century, the stove was in general use to burn either wood or coal.

More Inventions

Franklin improved the streetlight by fitting it with four panes of glass and piercing the top and bottom to allow for ventilation.

Among the other practical articles that Franklin invented were the library stepstool, a chair whose seat could be lifted and folded down to make a short ladder, and a mechanical arm for reaching books on high shelves. The same kind of mechanical arm

is still in use in some grocery stores. Franklin invented the rocking chair when he fitted the legs of his armchair with curved pieces of wood. He designed another type of chair with a broad arm on one side to provide a writing surface. Similar chairs are still used in many classrooms.

Franklin invented the odometer to measure distances along colonial roads used by the postal service. He also made a machine for generating static electricity.

Franklin even invented a musical instrument called an "armonica," which produced clear, bell-like tones using thirty-seven glass hemispheres. Unfortunately, the glass armonica never really caught on. The sounds it produced were beautiful, but the vibration of the glass upset the nerves of the musicians who played the instrument for any length of time and set their teeth on edge.

Franklin's "armonica"
was a mechanical form
of musical glasses.

4

The Public Servant

At the same time that Franklin was establishing himself as a successful printer and businessman, husband and father, and as an internationally renowned scientist, he was also embarking on a career in public life. His public services were many and varied.

By 1748, when he was forty-two, Franklin was able to turn his printshop over to others to manage. He could live comfortably off the income from the business. He was free to devote himself solely to the things that mattered to him—scientific research, family life, and public service. In that same year Franklin became a member of the Philadelphia City Council. He worked untiringly on projects to improve life in his adopted city and on ways to improve the administration of the colonies.

The Philosopher

Franklin's lifelong dedication to public service was the natural outgrowth of his personal philosophy: a person's highest duty in life is to serve others. At heart Franklin was primarily a philosopher. He was a seeker of knowledge and truth. He spent most of his life thinking about and studying the underlying principles and laws that govern the universe. In all things he attempted to discover the best course of action and to perfect the art of living.

Franklin believed in God the Creator of the universe, but he had doubts about some of the teachings of the Bible and Christianity. He believed more in the ethical teachings of religion than in its doctrines. Like many other eighteenth-century thinkers, Franklin was a deist. Deism was a faith based on reason, but at times it appeared cold and impersonal.

Deists believed that the complexity and grace of the natural world were enough to demonstrate the existence of God. Formal religion was attacked as a waste of time. Franklin believed that God and mankind were best served by good works.

Even with his busy life, Franklin did not neglect his personal developments. He always found time for self-improvement and study, especially in the areas of science and philosophy. He taught himself enough French and German to read these languages and to correspond with scientists abroad. He could also read Latin, Italian, and Spanish. And he continued to meet regularly with his friends in the Junto Club.

The Junto Club

The Junto Club started out as the Leather Apron Club. A "leather apron man" was the term given to a craftsman in the eighteenth century. Workers such as blacksmiths, shoemakers, carpenters, and printers were all eligible to join the club. The members were a group of tradesmen who worked for a living like Franklin himself. The name Junto means a group or society.

They met weekly in a tavern to discuss the important issues

of the day, their personal concerns, and to find ways to improve life for mankind. The Junto that Franklin started survives today in the American Philosophical Society, founded by the Club in 1743. Franklin and his friends in the Junto undertook to transform society by their philanthropic efforts and their projects for civic improvements.

The Library Company

Books were expensive in the eighteenth century and doubly so in the colonies, since they had to be imported from England. The Junto founded the Library Company of Philadelphia to pool their individual libraries and to accumulate funds to buy new books. In 1731 Franklin was one of the founders of the first public library in Philadelphia. The idea quickly spread to other northern cities.

In the eighteenth century the Bible was the book most universally read and studied. Works of poetry or collections of essays and fables were also popular. Light reading was practically unheard of; the writing of fiction had barely come into existence.

People who read books mostly concentrated on ancient Greek and Latin classics, both in their originals and in English translations. Knowledge of ancient languages was one mark of the extent of a gentleman's education. Other people read serious books on law, theology, and political theory.

The Philadelphia Academy

Franklin made efforts on behalf of public education. In 1749 he began to convince a group of prominent Philadelphia citizens to support the founding of an academy for the instruction of the city's youth. One of the first stipulations was that the academy should be free from any religious influences.

Franklin also believed that the study of the English language and its literature should be the basis of the curriculum. This was a radical idea in the eighteenth century, when it was expected that the classical languages, Latin and Greek, constituted the best possible subjects for study.

The Philadelphia Academy opened its doors in 1751 and in 1791 was incorporated as the University of Pennsylvania. Today the University is one of the leading centers of learning in the United States.

The Civic Franklin

Among civic improvements, Franklin and the Junto suggested that Philadelphia pave its streets. They originated plans for lighting the city and keeping the streets clean.

In 1736 Franklin's Philadelphia Volunteer Fire Department was the first in the colonies. Each member had his own leather bucket, and a bucket brigade was set up to help put out fires.

Franklin helped to organize Philadelphia's first police force. He also wanted to spread the British idea of insuring houses and property against fire and loss. Today the Franklin Insurance Company still has headquarters in Philadelphia!

Franklin raised funds for Philadelphia's first hospital, which was also the first hospital in the colonies. He also urged the colonies to build more lighthouses to guide ships at sea.

Franklin and
the American Postal System

Franklin was named postmaster of Philadelphia in 1737. Immediately he began to improve the postal system of the colonies. Before stamps were introduced, people who received mail had to

collect their mail at the post office and pay the postage, a fee assessed by the packet's weight. Because there was no way of advertising when mail had arrived and for whom, piles of unclaimed mail resulted in huge losses in revenue. Franklin established a system whereby a list of the names of people who had mail waiting for them was printed in the newspaper. Once they knew it was there, people were eager to collect their mail and pay the fees for it.

Between 1753 and 1774 Franklin served as deputy postmaster general of the American colonies. The inefficient postal system had been losing money for years. By 1756, under Franklin's direction, it was making a handsome profit. Later, as postmaster general, Franklin improved the quality of mail service throughout the colonies just as he had done in Philadelphia. He changed the methods of bookkeeping and instituted weekly mail service in areas where mail had been delivered only every few months.

A statue of Franklin at the University of Pennsylvania, Philadelphia, which he founded

Chapter

5

The Statesman

Franklin was appointed clerk of the Pennsylvania Assembly, the legislative body of the colony, in 1736. This was the beginning of his political career. He continued as clerk until 1751. Franklin was elected a member of the Assembly in 1750, and years later he would serve as its president. As his political influence grew stronger, Franklin's interests took him far beyond the needs of the city of Philadelphia and the colony of Pennsylvania.

Franklin the "Soldier"

During the French and Indian War, which lasted from 1744 to 1763, the British and the colonists needed to protect themselves from the joint threat posed by Indians and the French along the western frontier. Franklin did not take up the arms of a soldier himself, but he supported the British and colonial interests and helped organize companies of volunteer militia. Franklin himself led a military expedition into Pennsylvania's Lehigh Valley and helped to establish a chain of forts. He even directed the building of the fortifications that were to protect settlers at the frontier from French and Indian attacks.

The Albany Plan of Union

In 1754 the Albany Congress was held at Albany, New York. The Congress had been called to discuss the threat that the French and their Indian allies posed to the colonists' safety. Franklin served as the delegate from Pennsylvania and was joined by delegates from six other colonies. There he proposed a plan to unite the colonies.

Franklin's "Albany Plan" called for setting up an intercolonial council to provide a central government and a unified military command. The council was to be made up of forty-eight representatives drawn from the thirteen colonies. The representatives were to be elected by the individual colonial legislatures. The colony's wealth and population would determine the number of representatives it could send.

Franklin also proposed that the British monarch should appoint a president general to serve as a royal governor over all the colonies. His salary would be paid by the British government. He would preside over the council of representatives and have the power to veto the council's resolutions. The council would regulate Indian affairs and levy taxes necessary to build forts and to maintain an army.

Franklin's suggestions were approved by the delegates to the Albany Congress. But when the Albany Plan of Union was presented by the representatives in their individual colonial assemblies, it was promptly rejected. Opponents of the proposal feared that the plan would place too much emphasis on the colonies and relieve the British of their duty to protect them. The individual colonies would lose some of their power if they were subject to government by a council.

Franklin was disappointed that his vision of a central colonial government was not fulfilled. But the seeds had been sown, seeds that would later bear fruit. Franklin's dream of a unified government for the colonies was to become a reality some twenty years later when he served as a delegate to the Second Continental Congress. There the United States of America was born.

Braddock's Campaign

In 1755 Franklin aided the ill-fated campaign of General Edward Braddock by advancing 20,000 pounds of his own money to provide troop wagons and supplies. Fortunately, the British government later reimbursed him for his expenses.

Braddock commanded a force of well over 2,000 soldiers, of whom more than half were colonial volunteers. Braddock's army met with sudden defeat in an ambush about 10 miles (16 km) from the French stronghold of Fort Duquesne (in modern Pittsburgh). Two-thirds of Braddock's men died, including most of his officers. Braddock himself was mortally wounded.

The young George Washington, who had accompanied Braddock as an aide, complained that Braddock had secured the defeat of his army by unnecessary delays in its progress toward Fort Duquesne. General Braddock had asked Benjamin Franklin's advice before undertaking the campaign. Franklin had recommended a swift, decisive strike at the French fort. But the army had moved forward slowly as it built a road to move its supply wagons, giving the French ample time to prepare a surprise attack.

The disaster did have at least one hidden benefit, however.

The road that Braddock and his men had built opened up western Pennsylvania and the Ohio Valley to British settlers, a situation that Franklin heartily endorsed.

"Join, or Die"

The French and Indian War dragged on for several more years. Franklin continued to work for the victory of the British colonists by both his political efforts and his writings, published in newspapers and widely circulated pamphlets.

Franklin's own *Pennsylvania Gazette* carried the first political cartoon in an American paper, a landmark in the history of journalism. Franklin himself designed the famous woodcut entitled "Join, or Die" that shows a snake cut into several parts, each representing the separate colonies. He took a deep emotional interest in the welfare of the colonies and was overjoyed when news came in 1763 that the English and colonists had at last won the French and Indian War.

Franklin and Pennsylvania

By the middle of the eighteenth century Pennsylvania was a large and prosperous colony. Its population was largely an urban one centered around Philadelphia. Germans, Scots, Swedes, French Huguenots, Irish, and Jewish settlers were all part of the mixture of people who settled there.

Originally settled by Quakers, Pennsylvania still had a large Quaker population. Quakers were pacifists, opposed to war. They therefore were against military expenditures that were necessary to maintain the Indian frontier.

In addition, descendants of William Penn, the colony's Quaker

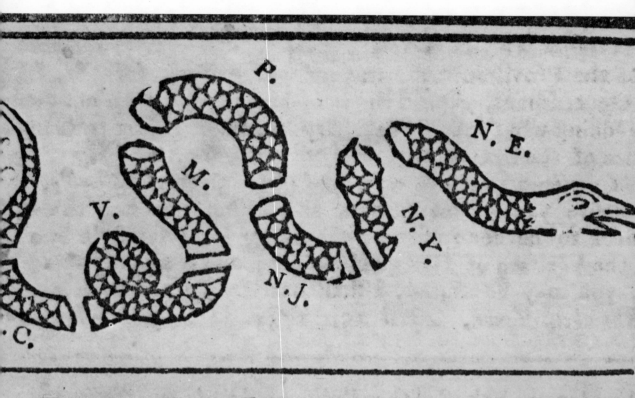

JOIN, or DIE.

Franklin believed that the states should
unite in both name and spirit.

founder, continued to hold a proprietary interest in the colony even though they were living in England. Most of the territory was still a private family estate, and members of the Penn family were exempt from taxation even though they were the largest landowners.

In 1757 Franklin found himself the leader of the political party opposed to the privileges of the Penns. Franklin went to England to testify against the Penns and to represent the colony's interests. In 1760 he won his case against them. The Pennsylvania colony now had the legal right to levy taxes on the lands owned by the Penn family. But Franklin recommended that the colonial legislature use restraint in taxing them. In 1762 he returned to America.

Protesting the Stamp Act

In 1764 Franklin returned to England, this time to protest the Stamp Act. The Stamp Act was the first direct tax that the British government imposed on the colonies. It required the Americans to pay a fee to affix an official stamp on virtually all documents and printed materials, including licenses, certificates, pamphlets, and newspapers. The revenue generated by the tax was to be spent on colonial defense.

As soon as the provisions of the Act were made known, public opposition was aroused. Businessmen and lawyers were among the most outspoken opponents of the tax, since it would greatly increase their costs of doing business. Franklin, too, as a printer, recognized that the fees would affect his own business. He urged repeal of the tax in Parliament in London, but his reasoned arguments fell on deaf ears.

Franklin had originally favored the substance of the act and had even had some of his friends appointed as collectors. But public opinion went against the Stamp Act very quickly, and Franklin, in a sharp about-face, changed his viewpoint. His initial support of the Act may have been one of the few misjudgments of his political career.

The central issue cited by the colonists was that they were freeborn English citizens whose colonial legislatures were responsible for passing laws and levying taxes. They had no representation in the English Parliament that wanted to impose the tax. "No taxation without representation" became the rallying cry. The colonists opposed the measure by boycotting English goods. Franklin debated long and hard against the tax, and in 1765 he had the satisfaction of seeing the Stamp Act repealed.

While still in England, between 1768 and 1770, Franklin was successively named agent for the colonies of Georgia, New Jersey, and Massachusetts at the British court. On this trip Franklin stayed in England for more than ten years. He was abroad for such a long time that he even considered making England his home.

Franklin the Transatlantic Citizen

On his several trips to and from England, Franklin became a skilled practitioner of what we might today call "shuttle diplomacy." Franklin was widely respected on both sides of the Atlantic and was skilled at getting people with opposing viewpoints to agree. He had to keep careful track of developments in England and the colonies. No single man could equal Franklin's deep knowledge and understanding of both countries. And no one had such an informed understanding of their characters and governments.

Franklin enjoyed his trips abroad enormously. They put him in touch with European culture and music during one of the continent's great golden ages of art and science. Franklin was able to mingle with the most brilliant and cultivated minds of the day. And the great and learned received Franklin as their equal, and everywhere he was presented with medals and honorary degrees.

Franklin Sours Against Britain

By 1775 Benjamin Franklin had been a loyal British subject most of his sixty-nine years. He had been present at the coronation of George III in 1760 and had hailed the king as a wise and benevolent ruler concerned with the welfare of all his subjects on both sides of the Atlantic. Franklin hoped to see America prosper within the family of the British Empire, but he gradually came to realize that Britain's king and government were pursuing a course that would not allow the colonies self-determination and self-respect.

It was with great bitterness and after agonizing contemplation and debate that Franklin turned his back on George III and on British rule in the colonies. Still, he always remained fond of the country of his forebears and believed in the ability of the British to organize, to colonize, and to get things done.

A series of events helped to turn Franklin from a loyal subject of the crown into a colonial patriot convinced of the need for American independence. Late in 1774 a scandal erupted over a series of letters written by Thomas Hutchinson, the royal governor of Massachusetts. The letters had been placed in Franklin's hands in confidence. Some people even suggested that Franklin had obtained the material by underhanded means. The letters cast the governor in an unfavorable light, as a betrayer of colonial interests.

Franklin circulated the letters in the hope of having Hutchinson removed from office, but his plan backfired and Franklin was made to appear unethical and unscrupulous in the eyes of the British government. Franklin suffered great humiliation when he appeared before the Privy Council in London and was called a thief for obtaining the letters improperly.

The Countries Move
Closer to War

The British branded Franklin as "the great fomenter of the opposition in America." He was stripped of the position of colonial postmaster general, and his arrest was even contemplated. The British government disliked Franklin because he had embarrassed the government and was helping to start the Revolutionary War that would deprive Britain of the thirteen colonies.

Franklin left England when it became clear that the British were preparing a case against him for treason. Had he been tried and convicted, he would have faced years of imprisonment and even possible execution. In the spring of 1775, as the countries moved closer to war, Franklin sailed for home, bitterly disappointed that he had failed to help keep the American colonies and the British Empire intact.

Chapter

6

The Patriot and Revolutionary

Next to George Washington, who commanded the American military forces throughout the Revolutionary War, Franklin was probably the most important of our founding fathers. His democratic philosophy and idealism spearheaded the drive for American independence. His gift of persuasion and his social graces helped win the moral and financial support of France. Without French help, the American colonists would have had a harder time fighting the British.

When Franklin left England in the spring of 1775, war between Britain and America seemed inevitable. He returned to Philadelphia to find his country at war. While Franklin was sailing across the Atlantic, the battles at Lexington and Concord had already been fought.

Even though Franklin had lost the favor of the British government, his return to the American colonies was marked by triumph, not disgrace. In the eyes of his countrymen he was a hero, because he had done much for the sake of his country.

The fledgling nation put Franklin to work right away. Franklin was renamed postmaster general for the colonies. He was also sent as one of three commissioners to gain support in Canada for the American Revolution, but most Canadians remained loyal to Britain. Colonists who sided with the British were known as Loyalists, while those who fought for American independence were called Patriots. Strangely enough, Franklin's son William was the royal governor of New Jersey, and he became one of the leaders of the Loyalist cause in America. This major political difference within the Franklin family was a source of great bitterness and embarrassment. For years afterward, and until shortly before Benjamin Franklin's death, father and son regarded each other as strangers.

In 1775 Franklin was named a delegate to the Second Continental Congress and served on many different committees. He was one of the originators of the plan—approved by the Second Continental Congress—for a unified government for the new nation formulated under the Articles of Confederation. He also helped draft a new constitution for Pennsylvania.

Franklin was originally asked to draft the Declaration of Independence, but Thomas Jefferson ended up doing most of the writing. Still, some of the wording of the Declaration is Franklin's own. Franklin also signed the Declaration. As he affixed his signature, Franklin is said to have joked: "We must all hang together

For the 150th anniversary of the signing of the Declaration of Independence, Norman Rockwell depicted Franklin signing his name.

or we shall all hang separately." But no one is certain that he actually said this famous line.

An American in Paris

The United States had an even bigger assignment in store for Franklin. He was persuaded to go to France to gather French support for the Revolutionary cause. In the autumn of 1776, Franklin, now seventy years old, found himself crossing the Atlantic once again, this time bound for France. It was not an easy trip for someone of Franklin's years who was also in poor health. Franklin suffered from gout, a disease that causes painful swelling of the joints, and several different skin infections. He also suffered from a painful condition caused by a kidney stone. Today the problem could probably be corrected by surgery or treatment, but Franklin had to live with it.

When he arrived in France he was suffering from a skin ailment that made his scalp itchy and scaly. To hide this fact he wore a coonskin cap. The French were so delighted to see Franklin looking like their conception of a North American trapper that he decided to continue wearing the fur hat after his skin had cleared up. He even had several portraits painted that show him wearing the hat. To ease his skin rashes and soothe his aching joints, he soaked for several hours a day in a hot bath drawn in a tub that was covered with a special lid that allowed him to work or to receive visitors!

The French Social Whirl

In France, Franklin lived at Passy, near Paris, in a house owned by a wealthy Frenchman. Elegant dinner parties, sparkling conversation, and flirtation with fashionable ladies were just a few of the distractions that Franklin found in Paris. He met with, dined with, and talked with all the great men of the age. Two of Franklin's grandsons stayed with him to keep him company and to assist him in his work.

Franklin found French society much to his liking. It was elegant, intellectual, and witty. In Paris Franklin met men and women who shared his interests in science and philosophy, people who praised him as a great scientist and statesman.

The French idolized Franklin because of his wit and intelligence. French people of fashion wanted portraits or busts of Franklin to decorate their rooms. Society ladies held meetings called *salons*, where the brilliant men of the day met to discuss events, politics, ideas, and the arts. All were eager to hear and meet Franklin.

Franklin fit in with the French society of the period because he was both a philosopher and a political activist. The French were experiencing one of the golden ages of civilization, the Enlightenment. The Enlightenment was a time of heightened political awareness, as men and women attempted to apply human intelligence to solving the problems of government. It was a time of great achievement in French literature and the arts. Philosophers were trying to reshape society according to the laws of reason and science.

Franklin stayed in France for several years and was welcomed everywhere as "Doctor" Franklin. One Frenchman praised Franklin with these inspired words: "He snatched lightning from the sky and the scepter from the tyrant." He won support and recognition and scored a personal triumph among French intellectuals. The vision of America as a wilderness paradise was an idea that appealed to the French.

The French—and other Europeans—observed what was going on in America with admiration and envy. The concerns of Americans, it seemed to them, were those of the Enlightenment. Americans cared about the education and cultivation of the individual, but not about sophistication and luxury. They had ideals, but practiced tolerance. They believed in reason, but also in compassion. They also believed in peace, but they were willing to fight for equality and freedom.

The American colonies were like an experiment in Enlightenment philosophy. The Americans were proving, against all odds, that right-thinking men and women could throw off the shackles of tyranny even when faced with an adversary as formidable as Great Britain. A few years later the French would themselves imitate the colonists and stage their own revolution. Only in that case the oppressors would be their own countrymen.

Franklin's Diplomacy Wins French Support

When Franklin arrived in France two other Americans, Arthur Lee and Silas Deane, were already there, trying to gain French support. They were joined for a time by John Adams, but their diplomatic efforts eventually failed.

Franklin spent more than a year seeking French backing for the American cause. By 1778 he had persuaded the French king, Louis XVI, to recognize the new government of the United States of America. Franklin's personality and the recent decisive victory of the American Patriots over General Burgoyne's troops at Saratoga in October 1777 won the respect of the French. They were convinced of the solidity of the American cause and ultimate victory in the war against the British.

Even before 1778 France had been unofficially helping the American colonies. Almost from the beginning of the war the French had been channeling money and materials secretly to the Americans through a make-believe importing firm known as Hortalez and Company that was funded by the kings of France and Spain. The formal recognition of the United States by the French king made this subterfuge no longer necessary. The French entered the war openly on the American side.

A treaty securing an alliance between France and the United States was signed on February 6, 1778. The principal goal of the treaty was to bring about the independence of the United States. The French and the Americans also made favorable trade agreements. France pledged that it would seek no additional territory in North America, and the Americans promised to protect France's interests in the French West Indies.

Deane and Lee were jealous of Franklin's diplomatic and personal successes and proved troublesome. They were dismissed by Congress, leaving Franklin the sole representative of the United States in France, and Franklin rose to meet the challenge.

Franklin masterminded much of the American war effort from his position in France. His effective administration helped turn the tide of the war. He bought and dispatched supplies, negotiated loans, gathered information, and recruited French army and navy battalions to send to America. He secured a ship for John Paul Jones, the American naval hero, named the *Bonhomme Richard*, in honor of the French title of Franklin's *Poor Richard's Almanack*.

Franklin secured virtually all the outside help the Americans received in the war. He encouraged French privateers to seize goods from British ships and was then responsible for redirecting their shipment to the American colonies. Europeans assisted the Americans in many ways. Adventurers paid their own passage to America to join the colonial forces, and wealthy aristocrats sent gifts of money and supplies.

Why Did France Help?

It may seem odd that Louis XVI supported the American revolutionary cause. The already bankrupt monarch willingly plunged himself further into debt on America's behalf. This may seem doubly odd since only twenty years earlier the Americans were fighting side by side with the British against the French in the French and Indian War over the rights to colonial territories in North America.

French support of the American war was a combination of lofty idealism and practical self-interest. Certainly there were philosophical reasons for French support. America had long served as an ideal of the unspoiled wilderness republic with a strong, free people. This was a favorite concept of the French Enlightenment.

But there were more practical reasons as well. France welcomed the chance to fight against the British, even indirectly. They did not want to risk a war close to home (and England is separated from France only by the English Channel, a mere 26 miles, or 42 km). But they saw the war in America as a way to further French interests by weakening Britain's imperial power.

France saw the American Revolution as a strategic move to enhance French security and to protect French markets in Europe and abroad. The French also welcomed the chance for revenge against the country that had recently defeated them in the French and Indian War and had taken French-Canadian holdings for itself in 1763. France was happy to engage George III's army in battle.

In 1778, Louis XVI's minister, the Comte de Vergennes,

In 1778 Benjamin Franklin signed the
Treaty of Amity of Commerce and of Alliance
between France and the United States.

hastened to sign the Franco-American alliance just eleven days before the British planned to begin a program of reconciliation with the American colonies. This was a deliberate attempt to make things difficult for England and even helped prolong the American conflict.

The War Is Over

After the fighting concluded with the British surrender at Yorktown, Franklin was the first to make contact with the British negotiators who had been sent to Paris from London. He was also the first to formulate terms of the peace between the United States and Great Britain, which officially ended the War of Independence. The groundwork for the treaty had already been laid when John Jay and John Adams arrived from America to help with the negotiations.

The terms of agreement that Franklin first presented were essentially the same as those that were finally endorsed in the Treaty of Paris in 1783. The alliance with the French, who maintained considerable land holdings in North America, gave weight to the United States' bargaining position.

The Treaty of Paris guaranteed complete independence for the new nation, and enforced evacuation of all British forces remaining in occupied territory. The treaty also defined the borders of the United States. The western boundaries of the United States that were agreed upon were to be the Great Lakes and the Mississippi River, a border contiguous with the French North American holdings, the Louisiana Territory.

The other terms of the settlement were designed to be fair to all parties. They included American fishing rights in the waters off the coast of British Newfoundland. The rights of both British and American ships to use the Mississippi River were established. The rights of loyal British subjects who had lost lands and other property or who had bad debts as a result of the war were guaranteed by new laws.

Franklin was particularly concerned about the fate of American prisoners of war, many of whom languished for years in English prisons. He gave his own money to make the American prisoners more comfortable and worked hard to secure their release.

Coming Home

Franklin had spent nine years in France. These years were among the happiest of his life. Both he and his hosts had many regrets when the time came for him to return to America. He could happily have spent the remainder of his days among the French, and many of his friends pressed him to stay on.

But the desire to return home proved stronger. His work of diplomacy completed, Franklin resigned as minister to France in 1785. He said his farewells and traveled on to England to stay with friends for a few days. Then he set sail for America. His arrival back in Philadelphia was greeted by happy throngs of people, parades, and speeches.

7

_Franklin and
the Constitution_

The Articles of Confederation

The major event of Franklin's later years was his participation in the Constitutional Convention that was held in Philadelphia during the long, hot summer of 1787. Franklin was not convinced of the need for the Convention, but certain plans for the government of the country had to be made. For one thing, the United States still lacked a president. And some leaders of the country who favored a strong central government believed that the Congress was merely limping along under the Articles of Confederation.

The Articles were the first American constitution. Franklin had been a member of the Second Continental Congress where the Articles had been hastily drawn up in 1776. They were adopted in 1781. Franklin did not really see the need for a new constitution. He did not press for the Constitutional Convention to be held.

Once the plans for the Convention were under way, however, Franklin was eventually included among the delegates, and he set to work wholeheartedly in support of the plans. He took his responsibilities as a delegate very seriously. He attended the meetings faithfully every day and paid close attention to all the proceedings. Already eighty-one years old, Franklin was the oldest member of the Convention.

George Washington was the actual presiding officer of the Constitutional Convention. But it was Benjamin Franklin who seemed to preside over the meetings as the spirit of wisdom embodied in America's foremost philosopher and statesman. Franklin's presence and his guidance were more important than any specific plans or wording that he contributed to the Constitution.

Franklin at the Convention

As always, Franklin came to a public gathering brimming with ideas which he presented with enthusiasm and backed up with solid arguments. Franklin had strong feelings and thoughts about all three branches of government: the legislative, the judicial, and the executive. Few of his favorite ideas for the Constitution met with any success.

The other delegates to the Constitutional Convention regarded Franklin as the honored elder statesman, a man to be venerated but not always listened to. They had their own ideas and reasoned that as great a man as Franklin had been, his remaining days were few and he no longer had any real power.

Factions, special interest groups, heated debates, and disagreements slowed the progress of the delegates and threatened to undo the work of the Convention. Many times Franklin's humor and cool head helped to soothe ruffled feelings among the delegates who were worn out by long days of discussion and debate.

Franklin's influence led the Constitutional Convention delegates to cooperate and to compromise. His self-assurance helped

Benjamin Franklin addressing the Constitutional
Convention, at which George Washington presided

prevent disruption and inspired confidence in the delegates that they could accomplish their task. Finally they began to work in earnest to hammer out their differences and to reach mutually satisfying agreements.

Solutions to the Problems

One of the biggest problems facing the Constitutional Convention was trying to forge a single nation out of what had been, essentially, thirteen separate states, or republics. Under the Articles of Confederation the rights of all states had been equal. Now there seemed little hope of reaching an agreement. There was a stalemate over whether the government should have a one-chamber or a two-chamber Congress.

The real issue was to ensure each state fair representation in Congress. The larger states—Massachusetts, Pennsylvania, and Virginia—felt that if each state had the same number of representatives, their larger populations would not be fairly represented. The smaller states reasoned that if population alone were the basis for representation in the government, then their needs and concerns would be overlooked.

The issue of unequal representation threatened to dissolve the Convention. Many delegates were ready to pack up and return to their home states without forming any agreement on the plan for a federal government. But a compromise was reached.

Franklin originally favored a single chamber for Congress. However, he finally came to see that a bicameral, or two-house, legislature, or Congress, would satisfy both large and small states. The Congress was to be made up of the House of Representatives, in which states are represented in proportion to their population, and the Senate, which has two representatives from each state, regardless of size or population. Eventually, Franklin and a committee of Convention delegates worked out the structure and responsibilities for each of the two houses. Helping to effect this compromise was one of Franklin's greatest contributions to the Convention.

Throughout the Convention, Franklin spoke in defense of democratic principles and of the rights of the common people. He favored placing the responsibility for bills involving money in the House of Representatives. He reasoned that "the people should know who had disposed of the money and how." He voted against writing a provision into the document requiring voters to own land or other property.

He thought that officials of the government should not receive salaries. He felt that this would encourage the legislature to be filled with more mature men, people who had already made their fortunes or who had been brought up in wealth and were consequently better educated. He reasoned that men who had no need of further enriching themselves would be less subject to corruption and bribery. British government officials had become notorious by abusing the power of their offices. Franklin wished to remove the incentive for men to run for office merely to enrich themselves.

He thought the president, or chief executive, should be eligible for one term only. He supported the idea that executive power should be shared among a council of men rather than rest with a single person, the president.

Among his recommendations for limiting the power of the executive branch, Franklin spoke out against giving the president power to cancel, or veto, the bills passed in the legislature. He spoke out in favor of the clauses in the Constitution that make the president subject to impeachment proceedings if he is accused of a crime.

The impeachment process ensures that the president is not

above the law and prevents him from assuming absolute power. And it gives the unjustly accused president a chance to be found innocent. An alternative way to remove a president, assassination, Franklin and the others found unacceptable. In that case, Franklin argued, ". . . the president is not only deprived of his life but of the opportunity of vindicating his character."

Finally, on the subject of the judicial branch of the government, Franklin thought that there might be a better way to choose judges than by legislative or executive appointment. The final resolution whereby the Supreme Court justices are chosen by the president remained a point of dissatisfaction in Franklin's mind.

The Document Is Finished

The Convention ran for four months, from May 22 to September 17, 1787. Franklin was present on each day of the session. On the last day of the Convention, the newly drafted Constitution was read aloud to the gathering. Franklin then handed a written statement to a secretary named Wilson to read for him. In it he summed up the proceedings.

Franklin's summary spoke plainly of his disapproval of some of the parts of the Constitution and of his disappointment that many of his own proposals were not embodied in the document. He believed that free men are bound to disagree on certain issues, but that compromise and acceptance are necessary for government and order. He graciously bowed to the will of the majority in these matters. He believed that the document was a good one and that time would prove the wisdom of the delegates' decisions:

> In these sentiments, Sir, I agree to this constitution with all its faults, if they are such. . . . I doubt too whether any other convention we can obtain may be able to make

a better constitution. For when you assemble a number of men to have the advantage of their joint wisdom, you inevitably assemble with those men all their prejudices, their passions, their errors of opinion, their local interests, and their selfish views. From such an assembly can a perfect production be expected? It therefore astonishes me, Sir, to find this system approaching so near to perfection as it does. . . . Thus I consent, Sir, to this Constitution because I expect no better, and because I am not sure that it is not the best. The opinions I have had of its errors I sacrifice to the public good.

Franklin's statement was regarded as a brilliant speech by the Convention delegates. Many of them asked for copies of it to use in persuading their own state legislatures to adopt the Constitution.

Finally Franklin moved that the Convention delegates sign the great document that they had just created. Thirty-eight of the delegates to the Convention then signed the Constitution.

The next day Franklin had the honor of presenting the new Constitution to the General Assembly of the Pennsylvania legislature, the first state government to become acquainted with the plan for the national government. This was the first step in the ratification process by which each state in turn endorsed and adopted the federal Constitution. A state convention, called for the purpose, ratified the Constitution for Pennsylvania on December 12, 1787.

Among Franklin's next activities was the attempt to secure lands for the capital of the new republic, which he hoped to see within the boundaries of his beloved Pennsylvania. However, Congress eventually settled on the District of Columbia, swampland on the Potomac River between Virginia and Maryland, to be the site of the nation's capital, Washington, D.C.

8

The Final Years

At home again in Philadelphia, Franklin was elected president of the Executive Council of the Commonwealth of Pennsylvania for three successive terms. Franklin spent his final years quietly, among his books and among his family and his friends. During this period he worked for various civil reforms in Philadelphia and campaigned for the abolition of slavery in the state of Pennsylvania. One of his last political acts was the signing of an antislavery resolution.

Franklin's Death

Franklin sensed that the end was near, but death seemed to hold no terror for him. He had already made his peace with God, and among his last words were these: "I am ready to repose myself securely in the lap of God and Nature, as a child in the arms of an affectionate parent."

Franklin died in his sleep the night of April 17, 1790. His daughter, Sally, and seven grandchildren were in the house with him.

Franklin's funeral was held a few days later. It was one of the greatest public events ever to be held in the newly founded nation. More than 20,000 people marched for miles, the largest crowd assembled to that date in America. All the clergy of Philadelphia—Protestant, Catholic, and Jewish—attended the ceremony, along with friends from near and far and swarms of the curious and appreciative. Franklin had been one of the great men of his age and one of the founding fathers of the great young nation.

Newspapers called the procession the biggest in Philadelphia's history. Members of Congress were among the throngs who joined Franklin's funeral procession to the churchyard. Franklin's body was buried next to that of his wife in Christ Church cemetery in downtown Philadelphia. The grave was marked soon after with a bronze plaque bearing this inscription:

The Body of
B. Franklin Printer
(Like the cover of an old book
Its contents worn out
And stript of its Lettering and Gilding)
Lies here, Food for Worms.
But the work shall not be lost,
For it will (as he believ'd) appear once more
In a new and more elegant Edition
Revised and corrected
By the Author.

Franklin had written the epitaph himself during a severe illness when he was twenty. He had thought he would die and had penned the humorous lines as he prepared himself for death. No other epitaph could seem more fitting.

In France many people observed a period of mourning or wore black armbands. In the United States, Congress declared a thirty-day period of mourning to honor the memory of a great man.

Benjamin Franklin was entirely a man of the eighteenth century. Many historians consider him *the* outstanding American of the colonial and early republic periods. He was equally well known in the Old and New Worlds. He was a man interested in everything, and he left the imprint of his powerful personality in such fields as education, journalism, literature, public administration, and humanitarian reform. His important contributions to American government and politics were surpassed only by his lasting contributions to science and philosophy.

For Further Reading

Bennett, Wayne. *The Founding Fathers.* Easton, MD: Garrard, 1975.

Daugherty, James. *Poor Richard.* New York: Viking, 1941.

D'Aulaire, Ingri and Edgar P. *Benjamin Franklin.* New York: Doubleday, 1950.

Eaton, Jeannette. *That Lively Man, Ben Franklin.* New York: Morrow, 1948.

Franklin, Benjamin. *The Autobiography of Benjamin Franklin.* (Many editions are available)

Fritz, Jean. *What's the Big Idea, Ben Franklin?* New York: Putnam, 1976.

Judson, Clara. *Benjamin Franklin.* Chicago: Follett, 1957.

Van Doren, Carl. *Benjamin Franklin.* New York: Viking, 1938.

Index